ANNUAL GIVING 101

♦

DR. MARIO L. HICKS

Copyright © 2023 Dr. Mario L. Hicks

All rights reserved. This publication, or any part thereof, may not be reproduced in any form or by any means, including electronic, photographic, or mechanical, or by any sound recording system, or by any device for storage and retrieval of information, without the written permission of the copyright owner.

Contents

────◆────

Chapter 1: Unleashing the Potential of Annual Giving.....5

Chapter 2: The Basics of Annual Giving..........10

    Fundraising Techniques and Best Practices..........12

    Annual Campaign Appeals..........15

    Developing a Strong Case for Support..........19

    Building a Robust Donor Pipeline..........20

Chapter 3: Annual Fund-Giving Strategy..........21

    Case for Support..........22

    Board Members..........25

Chapter 4: Using a Gift Table in Fundraising..........31

    Fill Out Your Gift Chart..........36

    Monitor and Update..........38

    Gift Table Dos and Don'ts..........40

Chapter 5: Leadership Giving..........43

    The Importance of Leadership Annual Giving..........46

Which Donors Are Candidates for Leadership Annual Giving? 47

Three Reasons Why Leadership Annual Giving is Essential 48

Getting Started with Your Program 49

Chapter 6: Giving Days 53

Peer-to-Peer Fundraising..59

Chapter 7: The Future of Annual Giving............64

Chapter 8: Putting It All 70

Chapter 1:
Unleashing the Potential of Annual Giving

In the vast realm of human experience, few endeavors can evoke profound joy, foster meaningful impact, and inspire transformative change, quite like the act of giving. Rooted deep within our collective consciousness, the instinct to give is a testament to our inherent compassion and empathy. Whether manifested through simple gestures, acts of service, or the provision of financial support, giving nourishes our souls and elevates the interconnectedness of our existence.

In philanthropy, annual giving stands as the foundation of hope and possibility. Serving as the lifeblood of charitable contributions, it pulsates with the rhythm of benevolence and is fueled by the spirit of generosity. Year after year, it breathes vitality into countless causes, organizations, and individuals, illuminating a path toward a brighter future.

Welcome, esteemed reader, to this enlightening journey of exploration and empowerment as we delve into the profound realm of annual giving and unlock its remarkable potential. Together, we shall embark upon an odyssey that transcends the mere transactional nature of financial contributions, unveiling the transformative power of regular, sustained giving.

Throughout the pages that lie ahead, we shall embark upon an expedition that surpasses the act of simply writing checks or making online donations. Our endeavor seeks to unravel the true meaning and purpose behind annual giving, thereby redefining it as a force accessible to all, regardless of financial means or social standing.

Annual giving is far from a solitary pursuit; it represents a collective movement, a symphony of goodwill conducted by individuals, communities, and organizations across the globe. We tend to focus so much on the major gifts that we forget where most of those major gifts started. The donor most likely started as an annual donor. Within these pages, you shall encounter extraordinary stories of ordinary individuals who have embraced the ethos of annual giving, forever altering the lives of those they touch. Through their tales of triumph, resilience, and unwavering determination, you will be inspired to embark on your own philanthropic voyage.

However, this book serves a greater purpose than simply recounting heartwarming anecdotes. It serves as a comprehensive roadmap, guiding you through the intricate landscape of annual giving and revealing the strategies, tools, and techniques necessary to amplify your impact and extend your influence. From the art of crafting compelling appeals to the science of harnessing cutting-edge technology, we will equip you with the knowledge and skills required to become a catalyst for positive change.

Furthermore, we shall explore the multitude of benefits that annual giving bestows upon the givers themselves. Extensive research has demonstrated time and again that giving is not merely an altruistic act; it is a powerful source of personal fulfillment, happiness, and even improved health. By embracing the principles and practices of annual giving, you can enhance your own well-being while creating a ripple effect that extends far beyond your immediate sphere of influence.

Nevertheless, we must acknowledge that this journey is not without its challenges. The landscape of annual giving is ever-evolving, shaped by societal shifts, technological advancements, and the fluid nature of human needs. In this book, we will navigate the complexities and address the obstacles that may arise, empowering you to adapt, innovate, and make a lasting impact in an increasingly dynamic world.

Together, let us embark on this transformative expedition—a voyage that will not only enrich your own life but also uplift the lives of countless others. As we explore the unparalleled potential of annual giving, may you uncover your own unique philanthropic purpose, one that aligns harmoniously with your passions and values. In doing so, you will join a vibrant community of changemakers united by the shared belief that we possess the power to shape a brighter future through our annual acts of kindness, compassion, and generosity.

With an open heart and an unwavering commitment to embracing the extraordinary within the ordinary, let us venture forth and unleash the boundless potential of annual giving.

Chapter 2:
The Basics of Annual Giving

Annual giving encompasses a nonprofit's efforts to receive donations and funds received for daily operations, ongoing projects and initiatives, and other activities for which an organization might not have a specific fund set aside. Essentially, annual giving describes a nonprofit or university's initiative to raise reliable yearly funding.

Annual giving is essential for nonprofits for several reasons:

1. **Provides a reliable source of income:** Annual giving provides a predictable stream of income that nonprofits can use to fund their ongoing operations, programs, and services. This helps organizations better plan and budget for their activities and ensures they can continue to deliver their mission sustainably.

2. **Builds and strengthens relationships with donors:** Annual giving allows nonprofits to engage with their donors regularly, which helps build and maintain relationships over time. By communicating with donors and showing them the impact of their contributions, nonprofits can strengthen their ties to

supporters and foster a sense of community around their mission.

3. **Increases awareness and support for the organization:** Through annual giving efforts, nonprofits can raise awareness of their mission and the impact of their work. By reaching out to donors and sharing stories of success, nonprofits can inspire more significant support for their cause and increase the visibility of their organization. An informed donor or volunteer can share your mission with passion and vigor.

4. **Helps to identify major donors:** Annual giving campaigns can help nonprofits identify potential donors by tracking giving patterns and identifying supporters who can give more. This can help organizations to build relationships with these donors over time and ultimately secure more significant gifts in the future.

Fundraising Techniques and Best Practices

There are a variety of fundraising techniques and best practices that nonprofit organizations can use to maximize their annual giving campaigns. Some of these techniques include:

1. **Direct Mail:** Direct mail is a traditional fundraising technique that sends letters, brochures, and other materials directly to potential donors. This approach can be effective, especially when combined with targeted lists and compelling messaging.

2. **Email Marketing:** Email marketing is a cost-effective way to reach a large audience of potential donors, especially younger donors who are more likely to engage with nonprofits through digital channels. To be effective, nonprofit organizations should segment their email lists and use personalized messaging that resonates with each donor.

3. **Online Giving:** Giving is an increasingly popular way for donors to donate to nonprofit organizations. This includes one-time and recurring donations, peer-to-peer fundraising campaigns, and crowdfunding platforms.

4. **Set your goals for the year:** How much is your nonprofit hoping to raise for its annual fund?

Calculate your current expenses plus ongoing projects as a starting point. Then, set an achievable goal while still striving to exceed your past fundraising totals.

5. **Identify prospective donors:** Annual giving is a great way to identify your most loyal donors, but when you're first starting your annual giving campaign, you'll have to segment who these potential loyal donors will be. Send your annual giving requests to previous donors and other types of supporters—such as volunteers and event registrants—as well.

6. **Create a compelling message:** Why should your supporters donate to your annual giving campaign? You should be able to answer this question before you launch your campaign. Remind supporters of your message and what specific projects and operations will be impacted by their donations.

7. **Personalize outreach:** Supporters provide data about their likes and interests when interacting with your nonprofit. What types of events are they attending? What causes and campaigns are essential

to them? Make sure to segment your outreach with the data and demographic information your nonprofit gathers.

8. **Make donating easy:** Optimize your online donation tools and donation forms to make giving simple for mobile and desktop users. If you're launching your campaign via email, include a link to your donation form. If you're sending direct mail, include a QR code on your donation page.

9. **Express appreciation for donors:** As with any other type of gift, let your donors know how much their donation impacted your organization. Keep your donors updated with information about what the annual giving campaign specifically funds, and always make sure to send a thank you message, whether in the form of an email, a postcard, or a text message.

Annual Campaign Appeals

Appeals are direct communication pieces to your prospects and donors via print or electronic delivery. They contain powerful content and create exposure for your organization by educating others on your past, current and future efforts. These solicitations generate awareness of your mission, build relationships, and increase revenue. Some common appeals are Mid-year, the Day of Giving, and the Season of Giving.

- **Mid-year** – Typically distributed in June or July, the Mid-year appeal is best sent via direct mail and electronic delivery. Sending out an appeal Mid-year will not affect planned year-end efforts.

- **Day of Giving** – A Day of giving is digitally driven. Every year a nonprofit or community will host a campaign to bring awareness to a mission, often with solid messaging on social media.

- **Season of Giving**– Promote your end-of-year throughout the month of December, electronically and through direct mail.

While you can shape your appeal in many ways, highlighting an individual situation or story will have the most impact by enhancing your donors' understanding and increasing their connection to your cause. Once messaging is complete and you've crafted a story, ensure the solicitation is delivered in a simple, informative, connective, and uplifting way. Here are some important tips you should consider:

- **Delivery** – Ensure the message is vibrant and concise. Use simple verbiage and keep statistics to a minimum. Statistics are great motivators but can also alter the voice of an appeal. Readers need to understand the message to connect to it easily. A confused donor will disregard an appeal, resulting in no gift.

- **Mission** – The voice of your appeal must prominently support your mission throughout the piece. Your organization's mission and objectives should be clear to the reader. If the design allows, directly state your mission on the appeal.

- **Personalization** – Personalization is critical to making donors feel important and connected to your cause. Simple additions such as the donor's name, last donation date, and the amount of their last gift can have a lasting impact. Personalization is a must for all major gift solicitations.

- **Imagery** – People naturally look at pictures before reading text. Capitalize on this by using images to tell your story and enhance the donors' emotions. Select photos that invoke empathy and joy to develop the drive and energy to support your cause. Comparative pictures (before and after) work well to achieve this.

- **Donor Impact** – Donors like to feel connected and valuable to the causes they believe in. Focusing on donor impact creates ownership and connection, ultimately increasing giving. Explain how donor support is critical to your mission, and highlight donor impact in your story.

- **Donation Amounts** – Engage your donors by showing and telling them how you use their money. Add increments to the end of your appeal because dollar amounts are connected to a tangible impact guide understanding what donors can influence. Keep amounts and explanations simple and use examples.

- **Convenience** – Accessibility is vital; make giving easy for your donors. Your website should reflect your current campaign; your donation button or page must be obvious. Include options, such as recurring gifts so that donors can give again automatically. Direct mail appeals should include a return envelope. It's no secret that social media is incredibly effective: Don't forget to include a link that leads directly to your donation page. Donors have little patience; if it's difficult to donate, your organization will miss out on funds.

- **Execution** – Appeals are endorsed by many people in many ways. Leadership and development are the mainstays of appeals, but other staff, board members, and volunteers must work collectively to drive the effort. In addition to face-to-face connections, appeals can be sent via email, promoted on social media, introduced by phone, and mailed directly to donors.

Developing a Strong Case for Support

Developing a strong case for support is another critical component of building an effective annual giving program. This involves articulating the organization's mission, vision, and values and demonstrating the impact of its programs and services on the community it serves. By developing a compelling case for support, nonprofit organizations can inspire donors to give and demonstrate the importance of their contributions. The case for support needs to have a call to action that is not in a negative voice. Donors do not want to save you from problems. Instead, they want to be on the winning team and join in on the success of your nonprofit.

Building a Robust Donor Pipeline

Building a robust donor pipeline is also critical to the success of an annual giving program. This involves identifying and cultivating various donors, from individual donors to corporate and foundation partners. By building solid relationships with donors, nonprofit organizations can create a loyal and engaged base of supporters committed to the organization's mission and values.

In this chapter, we've explored the basics of annual giving best practices, including setting clear goals, developing a solid case for support, building a robust donor pipeline, and using effective fundraising techniques and best practices. By focusing on these critical components, nonprofit organizations can build successful annual giving programs that support their mission and positively impact the community they serve. In the following chapters, we will dive deeper into these areas, providing practical tips and insights that will help you build an effective annual giving program for your organization.

Chapter 3:
Annual Fund-Giving Strategy

As a nonprofit organization, you rely heavily on the generosity of your donors to support your programs and initiatives. One key element of your fundraising efforts is the annual fund, which provides critical unrestricted support to help you meet your day-to-day needs and continue positively impacting your community. But with so many worthy causes vying for donors' attention, how can you ensure that your annual fund stands out and attracts the support it deserves? This guide explores practical strategies for maximizing your annual fund giving and engaging donors meaningfully.

Case for Support

An annual fund-giving strategy starts with a case for support. To create a compelling case for support, you must use a combination of emotional and factual storytelling to engage and inspire your readers. Here are seven essential components to include in your case statement:

1. **An Emotional Opening:** Your opening paragraphs should be attention-grabbing and emotionally evocative. Avoid starting with dry facts or statistics; instead, use a story to convey the need your

organization is addressing. A powerful opening will hook the reader and motivate them to continue reading.

2. **Your Mission and Vision:** After you've captured your reader's attention with an emotional opening, you need to articulate your mission and vision clearly. Explain why your organization exists and what you hope to achieve. Use bold language to convey your big vision and inspire donors to support your cause.

3. **Explanation of Your Programs**: In this section, you should describe your organization's programs and services in clear, easy-to-understand language. Avoid using technical jargon or insider terms that might confuse readers. Focus on what you do and how you help people in need.

4. **History of the Organization:** This section should give readers some background on your organization's history and accomplishments. Include information on the organization's founding and highlight any major milestones or achievements. If

you're a new organization, explain why you were created and who is involved in your leadership.

5. **Outcomes, Stories, and Proof of Impact:** This section should highlight your organization's impact on the community. Use testimonials and stories from clients, community leaders, and supporters to illustrate the difference your organization has made. Use statistics and charts to quantify your impact and show donors the tangible results of their contributions.

6. **Financial Needs**: You must outline your organization's funding needs. Be specific about how much money you need to raise and what it will be used for. Break down the costs of specific programs or projects to give donors a clear idea of how their contributions will be used. Consider including giving levels to give donors an idea of what their donation can accomplish.

7. **Means of Support:** You need to explain how donors can financially support your organization. This could include annual giving campaigns, major donor programs, planned giving opportunities,

monthly giving programs, or online donation options. Make it easy for donors to give by providing clear instructions on donating.

Remember, your support case should be organized around emotional and mission-focused headings. Use a combination of storytelling and data to convey the importance of your organization's work and motivate donors to act.

Board Members

When individuals join a nonprofit's Board of Trustees, they accept both a governing and fiduciary role, and part of their responsibility includes regularly reviewing the organization's financials. As fundraisers, we should lean on the board and ask them to step up and show their leadership by demonstrating their belief in the organization's mission and philanthropy's role in ensuring its success.

One way for the board to demonstrate their commitment is by advocating for the annual fund and sharing the case for support with their peers. They can talk about the impact of annual giving on the organization and encourage others to contribute. While achieving 100 percent participation from the board is a nice goal, focusing on sacrificial and pace-setting giving is essential.

A high-performing annual fund typically receives 20 to 25 percent of the total from trustees. If your board is meeting this benchmark, it's important to highlight their achievement and encourage them to do even more. However, if your board isn't meeting this benchmark, it is time to call upon them for increased support.

Encourage the board to think about why they should make a gift, especially an increased one, at a certain level. Is it because they just joined the board, it's a reunion year, or their child is in the final year in the school? By targeting top prospects within the board and making specific asks, the annual fund can reach its goals and continue to impact the organization positively.

Overall, the board can play a critical role in the success of the annual fund. By encouraging their leadership and support, the organization can continue providing exceptional community support.

Here is a sample case for support for a nonprofit organization that focuses on providing educational opportunities for underprivileged youth:

An Emotional Opening: Every day, countless young people are denied access to the educational opportunities they deserve. These children face incredible challenges and obstacles that prevent them from reaching their full potential. But we believe every child deserves the chance to succeed, regardless of background or circumstances. That's why our nonprofit organization is dedicated to providing educational opportunities to underprivileged youth in our community. With your help, we can create a brighter future for these young people and give them the tools they need to succeed.

Our Mission and Vision: Our mission is simple: to empower underprivileged youth through education. We believe education is the key to breaking the cycle of poverty and providing children with a brighter future. Our vision is to create a world where every child can access the educational resources and opportunities they need to thrive.

Explanation of Our Programs: Our organization offers a variety of programs designed to support underprivileged youth in our community. These programs include after-school tutoring, mentorship programs, college preparation workshops, and scholarship opportunities. We work with local schools and community organizations to identify students who require our services and support them to succeed.

History of Our Organization: Our organization was founded in 2005 by passionate educators who wanted to make a difference in the lives of underprivileged youth. Over the years, we have helped thousands of students achieve their goals and realize their potential. We are proud of our track record of success and are committed to continuing our work for years to come.

Outcomes, Stories, and Proof of Impact: We have seen firsthand the incredible impact our programs can have on the lives of young people. One of our students, John, came to us struggling in school and lacking confidence in his abilities. Through our tutoring program and mentorship opportunities, John was able to turn his grades around and gain the skills he needed to succeed in college. Today, John is a successful business owner and attributes much of his success to the support he received from our organization.

Financial Needs: We need your support to continue our work and provide educational opportunities to more underprivileged youth in our community. Our organization relies on the generosity of donors like you to fund our programs and make a difference in the lives of young people. We seek to raise $500,000 to fund our programs for the coming year. This money will expand our tutoring program, provide more scholarship opportunities, and reach needy students.

Means of Support: There are many ways to support our organization and help us empower underprivileged youth through education. You can make a one-time donation, become a monthly donor, or even volunteer your time and talents to help us achieve our mission. Every donation, no matter how small, makes a difference and helps us create a brighter future for young people in our community.

The Ask: We hope you will join us in our mission to provide educational opportunities to underprivileged youth. Together, we can make a difference in the lives of young people and create a brighter future for our community.

It is crucial to emphasize that your case for support should highlight your organization's current goals and convey the potential for expansion and long-term success. Donors want to feel confident that their contributions will be used well and that your organization has a clear growth plan. By outlining the big ideas and innovative strategies that your organization will use to achieve its mission, you can inspire donors to invest in your cause. Additionally, it is essential to emphasize the immediate impact that each donation will have, showing donors how their gifts will make a tangible difference in the lives of those your organization serves. A compelling and comprehensive case for support can be a powerful tool to engage donors and inspire them to become long-term supporters of your organization.

Chapter 4:
Using a Gift Table in Fundraising

A gift table is a fundraising tool that can track and manage various amounts of donations. This tool can help non-profit organizations plan their fundraising campaigns and maximize donations. Gift tables are commonly used for capital campaigns, annual fund drives, and other major fundraising efforts.

The gift table typically includes several columns with varying donation amounts in each row. The table is organized by size and number of gifts received, with the largest donations at the top and the smallest at the bottom. The total amount raised is tallied at the bottom of the table.

When creating a gift table, it is important to set realistic goals and consider the size and scope of the fundraising campaign. The table should also be tailored to the specific donor audience being targeted. For example, a campaign targeting major donors may have higher gift levels listed on the table than one targeting a broader base of supporters.

A gift table is an effective tool for tracking progress during a fundraising campaign. It helps identify which gift levels are most popular and which may need more attention. This information can be used to adjust the campaign strategy and tactics to meet fundraising goals.

Another benefit of using a gift table is that it can help to identify potential leadership donors. These donors give at the highest levels and may be interested in taking on a more active role in the fundraising campaign. Identifying and cultivating these donors can help to create a sense of ownership and investment in the campaign and increase the likelihood of its success.

In addition to tracking donations and identifying potential leadership donors, the gift table can also recognize and steward donors. Organizations can publicly acknowledge donors who have given at various gift levels, which can encourage others to give as well. This recognition can take the form of newsletters, annual reports, events, or other forms of public recognition.

Overall, the gift table is a valuable tool for any fundraising campaign. It can help to track progress, identify potential leadership donors, and recognize and steward donors. By using this tool, organizations can increase their fundraising success and achieve their goals.

Here is a step-by-step guide on how to use a gift table in fundraising:

1. **Determine your fundraising goal:** The first step in creating a gift table is to determine your fundraising goal. You need to know how much money you need to raise to achieve your goals.

2. **Divide your fundraising goal into gift levels:** Once you have set your fundraising goal, you must divide it into gift levels. Gift levels are the various dollar amounts donors can give to your organization. Gift levels should be meaningful and reflect the donor's gift's impact on your organization.

3. **Determine the number of gifts needed for each gift level:** After you have established gift levels, you need to determine the number of gifts you need at each level. For example, you may need ten gifts of $5,000 to reach your goal of $50,000.

4. **Identify potential donors for each gift level:** Once you know how many gifts you need, you can identify potential donors who can give at that level. You can do this by looking at your donor database or researching potential donors.

5. **Assign prospects to gift levels:** After identifying potential donors, assign them to gift levels based on their capacity to give. You can use a variety of factors to determine capacity, such as past giving history, wealth indicators, and personal connections.

6. **Develop cultivation and solicitation strategies for each gift level:** With your prospects assigned to gift levels, you can now develop cultivation and solicitation strategies for each level. Cultivation strategies may include personal visits, event invitations, or personalized communication. Solicitation strategies may include direct mail, phone calls, or face-to-face meetings.

7. **Track progress and adjust as necessary:** As you begin soliciting gifts, track your progress towards each gift level. Adjust your strategies as necessary based on donor response and feedback.

By following these steps, you can create a gift table that will help guide your fundraising efforts and increase the likelihood of achieving your fundraising goal.

Fill Out Your Gift Chart

If you haven't used spreadsheet formulas, this is an excellent opportunity to do so to build out your gift chart quickly and efficiently. Ideally, you build a chart that allows you to adjust as gifts come in over the year. Your completed chart should look similar to this:

Giving Targets	# of Donors Needed	Total Giving	# of Prospects Needed	# of Prospects Identified	Prospect Delta
$10,000	5	$50,000	50	42	-8
$5,000	10	$50,000	100	72	-28
$2,500	25	$62,500	250	245	-5
$1,000	40	$40,000	400	700	300
$500	100	$50,000	1,000	1,250	250
$250	250	$62,500	2,500	5,000	2,500
$100	500	$50,000	5,000	6,125	1,125
$50	1,000	$50,000	10,000	11,000	1,000
$25	2,500	$62,500	25,000	28,000	3,000
Less Than $25	Many	$22,500	Many	25,000	Many
	4,430	$500,000	44,300	77,434	8,134

This chart has a 10:1 ratio for donors to prospects. Ratios may vary by organization. A 5:1 prospect-donor ratio means an organization must engage with five prospects to generate one new donor. This ratio is commonly used as a benchmark for estimating the potential number of donors an organization can generate from its pool of prospects. It is important to note that this ratio can vary depending on the specific circumstances of each organization, such as the size of the donor pool, the effectiveness of fundraising tactics, and the nature of the donor base. A higher prospect-donor ratio may suggest a need to improve fundraising tactics or expand the donor pool. A lower ratio may indicate a strong donor base and an effective fundraising strategy. Ultimately, the prospect-donor ratio can be useful for organizations to evaluate the effectiveness of their fundraising efforts and adjust their strategies as needed.

Here are some tips on how to create this:

1. Begin by assessing your overall fundraising goal for the year. Determine the total amount of money you need to raise from donations to meet this goal.

2. Next, evaluate your giving database to determine the number of donors you currently have and the amount of money they typically give. Calculate the ratio of donors to dollars raised and use this ratio to estimate how many donors you will need to reach your overall fundraising goal.

3. Consider any new prospects you have identified through your targeting exercise. Add these prospects to your total number of potential donors.

4. Look at the distribution of donors across different giving levels. Determine whether you have enough donors at each level to reach your fundraising goal. If there is a shortfall at any level, you must adjust the number of donors needed to meet that level.

5. Finally, assess any opportunities to increase giving at the highest giving levels. Consider asking your board or major donors to make stretch gifts to help bridge any gaps in your fundraising plan. Adjust the number of donors needed at each level to ensure your overall fundraising goal is achievable.

Monitor and Update

Monitoring and updating your fundraising pyramid is crucial to ensure that you are on track to reach your fundraising goals. As donations come in, update your pyramid to reflect the additional gifts. To help you keep track of progress, consider adding columns to your spreadsheet to monitor and measure against your original assumptions. These columns may include:

- **What you have raised to date:** This column will show the total amount of money raised in your campaign. It will help you track progress toward your overall fundraising goal.

- **What you still need to raise:** This column will show the remaining money you need to raise to reach your goal. This can help you identify any shortfalls in your fundraising efforts and adjust your strategy accordingly.

- **Donors to date:** This column will show the total number of donors who have contributed to your campaign. This can help you track your outreach efforts' effectiveness and identify improvement areas.

- **Donors still needed:** This column will show the number of donors you need to reach your fundraising goal. This can help you identify which giving levels need more attention and adjust your outreach strategy accordingly.

By regularly updating these columns, you will have a clear picture of your progress and be able to make informed decisions about your fundraising strategy moving forward.

Gift Table Dos and Don'ts

- Start with a base gift amount by multiplying each person's or family's most recent gift by 1.25 and rounding to match the giving levels in your table. This helps you establish a starting point for your gift table and ensures consistent giving levels across all donors. Remember that this is just a starting point, and you may need to adjust amounts based on other factors such as donor capacity or giving history.

- Look at the historical giving patterns of donors and identify those who have increased their giving year over year to consider whether stretch gift amounts may be possible. This can help you identify donors who may be willing and able to increase their giving to your organization. Stretch gift amounts should be challenging but achievable, and you should always approach donors with respect and sensitivity to their financial situation.

- Use screening to identify a donor's giving capacity and their most significant gift to other nonprofits. Consider raising the ask amount further if there is a significant gap between what a donor is giving to your organization and what they are giving elsewhere. Screening can provide valuable insights into a donor's financial situation and philanthropic interests. Using this information, you can make more informed decisions about how much to ask for and how to position your organization's case for support.

- Update your monthly spreadsheet to track progress and share success reports with leadership and the board. Regular updates help you stay on top of your fundraising goals and make adjustments as needed. It's also important to share progress reports with key organizational stakeholders to keep them informed and engaged in fundraising.

- Don't be afraid to iterate and adjust your plan as needed throughout the year, including updating the number of prospects based on responses at each giving level. Fundraising is an iterative process, and you will likely need to adjust as you go along. Be open to feedback and willing to adjust your plan based on what you learn from donors and other stakeholders. Being flexible and responsive can increase your chances of success and build stronger relationships with your donors.

The key to any great campaign is information. Allow the gift table to drive your giving strategy. The more you know about your prospects and donors, the better you can curate your message, figure out how to ask for it and determine the best way to stand out and reach these donors.

Chapter 5:
Leadership Giving

Leadership Annual Giving can be defined as a giving program that focuses on securing donations ranging from $1,000 to $25,000. However, the specific donation amount that qualifies as a leadership gift may vary depending on the institution and its constituent base. For instance, some institutions may consider a gift of $5,000 or $10,000 as a leadership gift.

The most common example of leadership giving is the President's Circle, which typically requires a minimum donation of around $1,000. Major gift officers, on the other hand, are responsible for working with donors who have the capacity to give at least $25,000.

While fewer in number than major gift officers, leadership annual giving officers can be incredibly effective. Research indicates that 48% of prospects assigned to a leadership annual giving officer donate to the annual fund, compared to only 40% of assigned donors who make major gifts.

Leadership Annual Giving programs are essential to an institution's fundraising strategy. These programs help to identify prospects for major gifts, provide a bridge between annual giving and major giving initiatives, and offer an opportunity to cultivate lasting relationships with donors.

With a focus on personalized communication and attention to detail, leadership annual giving officers can be critical in securing funding for an institution's annual operations and future growth.

The foundation of your yearly giving program is rooted in leadership contributions. In the past, teams in charge of annual and major giving have often competed for donors. Without requiring major gift officers to incorporate an annual giving appeal into their strategy (which I highly recommend), annual giving teams may lose their top donors when they transition to major giving. While everyone strives to meet their goals and benefit the institution, this transfer can be difficult.

Typically, alumni relations aim to engage a wide range of people, annual giving teaches dedicated alumni about why the institution deserves their charitable contributions (at any level), and major giving provides individual attention to donors with the inclination and financial means to make significant gifts. Moving from the annual giving donor experience to the major giving donor experience can be a significant shift.

The Importance of Leadership Annual Giving

An integrated leadership annual giving program bridges the gap between annual giving and major giving initiatives. This program is designed to create a seamless transition for donors and prospects who are considering moving from annual giving to major giving. It is a key component in fostering cross-functional cooperation within an institution.

By incorporating leadership in annual giving, institutions can ensure that annual giving and major giving teams work together cohesively instead of competing for donors. Leadership annual giving programs are tailored to provide a personal touch to donors with a significant affinity and capacity for giving, thereby encouraging donors to increase their giving levels.

The benefits of a leadership annual giving program extend beyond just retaining donors. It is also an opportunity to identify and cultivate major gift prospects from a pool of annual donors. This allows institutions to build lasting relationships with their donors and prospects, leading to continued and increased support in the future.

Which Donors Are Candidates for Leadership Annual Giving?

Leadership annual giving programs can encompass donors moving up the pipeline towards major giving and those who have already made a significant major gift but can now give annually.

In addition to securing annual gifts, leadership annual giving officers play a crucial role in identifying prospects for major giving and discovering new opportunities for endowed scholarships and planned gifts. They are often the first point of contact for emerging donors, serving as the initial step in developing a lasting philanthropic relationship.

Research suggests that institutions with the healthiest pipeline of donors prioritize discovery visits, which account for at least 30%-35% of their visits. Leadership Annual Giving officers can help alleviate this burden for major giving teams, as they are well-equipped to qualify donors for major gifts and identify potential opportunities.

Three Reasons Why Leadership Annual Giving is Essential

1. **Retain Valuable Donors:** The gap between annual and major giving can create a disconnected donor experience. Without a clear transition from one giving level to another, loyal and consistent donors may feel overlooked or forgotten. Leadership annual giving programs help bridge this gap by providing a smooth transition between the two levels, ensuring that important donors maintain contact with your institution. This, in turn, helps to retain their support and build long-lasting relationships.

2. **Build a Pipeline for Major Gift Donors:** Major gift donors are now an older and smaller group than before. This means attracting emerging prospects to build a sustainable pipeline for major giving is essential. Leadership annual giving can help rejuvenate the ranks of major gift donors by engaging donors who can give more but may not yet be ready for a major gift. They can gradually move up the giving ladder while feeling appreciated and valued.

3. **Foster Career Progression for Fundraising Staff:** Experienced and engaged staff tend to be better fundraisers, which is why high turnover can significantly impact fundraising results. A strong leadership annual giving program can help create a clear career pathway for staff, from annual giving to leadership annual giving and then to major giving. This provides staff opportunities for growth, development, and recognition, which can boost their retention and performance. It also helps institutions build a strong team of skilled fundraising professionals committed to the institution's mission and vision.

Getting Started with Your Program

A leadership-giving society can play a vital role in the success of a nonprofit organization or university. By recognizing and engaging donors who contribute at higher levels, a giving society provides tangible benefits to its members and fosters a sense of community and loyalty. Furthermore, a well-run leadership giving program can help build a pipeline of major gift donors and lay the groundwork for future capital campaigns.

Review the list of steps needed to get your giving society going:

1. Create membership levels and benefits that focus on creating transformative member experiences.

2. Develop effective giving society member materials and publications, such as newsletters, e-newsletters, welcome kits, or special inserts in existing publications.

3. Develop a process for society renewals yearly, focusing on retention, upgrading, and preventing membership lapsing.

4. Monitor progress yearly and develop a specialized renewal process for lapsed giving society members.

5. Identify segments of members and donors who can be targeted for potential upgrades to higher giving society levels each year.

6. Identify special event donors who may qualify for giving society membership and build a membership

recruitment component into existing and future special events.

7. Aim to identify donors and members on the cusp of qualifying for membership and inspire upgrading to reach the giving society membership level benchmark.

8. Solicit giving society members as part of the annual fund special appeals.

9. Utilize gatherings and receptions to create exclusivity and inspiration for prospects to become engaged in the giving society.

10. Develop corresponding appeals with consistent messaging for social media and an online presence via the website, promoting giving society membership and benefits.

11. Utilize the giving membership society to inspire major gifts to the organization through the organization's major gift program.

12. Consider developing a Sustainer (monthly giving) Program as part of its membership.

13. Develop specialized recognition opportunities for the giving society, including recognition events, the annual report listing, plaque, etc.

14. Develop key metrics for giving society membership, including goals for increasing membership, renewals, retention, upgrades, inquiries, etc. Analyze and report on key metrics, making decisions on a strategy based on past and current results.

It is crucial to build a pipeline of major gift donors through leadership giving to ensure the success of your program. A strong annual fund is essential, but having a strong army of leadership donors ready to take the next step will be even more critical when your non-profit or university embarks on a capital campaign in the future. By investing in leadership annual giving, you can lay the foundation for a successful major gift program and secure the long-term sustainability of your organization.

Chapter 6:
Giving Days

Giving Days have recently become a popular fundraising strategy for nonprofit organizations and educational institutions. These events are usually short-term campaigns that encourage supporters to make donations within a specific timeframe, typically 24 hours or less. The rise of online platforms has made it easier for organizations to host Giving Days and reach a wider audience.

Online platforms have revolutionized the way nonprofits and educational institutions fundraise. These platforms allow organizations to create custom fundraising pages, accept donations, and track progress in one place. Giving Days have leveraged these capabilities to create a sense of urgency and excitement around fundraising efforts.

Giving Days are particularly effective because they inspire supporters to rally around a specific cause or campaign. By creating a designated day for giving, organizations can generate a sense of community and momentum around their fundraising efforts. Using online platforms allows for easy sharing on social media, which can help spread awareness and encourage more donations.

One of the key benefits of Giving Days is the ability to reach new donors. The time-limited nature of these campaigns can encourage people to give, who may not have done so otherwise. Additionally, online platforms make it easy for organizations to collect data on donors, such as contact information and giving history. This information can be used to create personalized follow-up strategies and foster ongoing relationships with donors.

To have a successful Giving Day, it is essential to plan strategically. This includes setting fundraising goals, determining the messaging and theme for the campaign, and identifying key audiences and communication channels. To promote the event, online platforms can create custom landing pages, social media posts, and email campaigns.

During the Giving Day itself, it is essential to keep supporters engaged and motivated. This can be done through live updates on progress, shoutouts to top donors, and gamification strategies such as challenges or competitions. You must have a strong system in place for collecting and processing donations and acknowledging and thanking donors. Here are important tips you should consider:

1. **Set a goal:** Determine a specific fundraising goal for your Giving Day, and communicate it clearly to your team and supporters.

2. **Build a team:** Recruit volunteers and staff members to help plan and execute your Giving Day. Assign specific roles and responsibilities to each person.

3. **Develop a communications plan:** Create a comprehensive plan for promoting your Giving Day. This plan should include social media posts, email campaigns, press releases, and other promotional materials.

4. **Create a landing page:** Create a landing page on your website specifically for your Giving Day. This page should include information about your organization, your fundraising goal, and how to donate.

5. **Create a toolkit for supporters:** Develop a toolkit that supporters can use to help promote your Giving Day. This toolkit should include sample social media posts, email templates, and other resources.

6. **Secure matching gifts:** Work with corporate sponsors and major donors to secure matching gifts

for your Giving Day. These matching gifts can help encourage more donations and increase your fundraising total.

7. **Host events:** Host events throughout the day to engage donors and build excitement. This can include virtual events like webinars and live streams and in-person events like donor receptions and meet-and-greets.

8. **Thank donors:** Be sure to thank donors throughout the day and after the event. This can include personalized thank-you emails, social media shoutouts, and other forms of recognition.

9. **Follow up:** Follow up with donors after the Giving Day to keep them engaged and informed about your organization's work. This can include newsletters, impact reports, and other forms of communication.

10. **Analyze results:** Analyze the results of your Giving Day to identify what worked well and what could be improved for next year. Use this information to inform your future fundraising efforts.

A giving day is great for several reasons:

1. **Generating immediate funding:** Giving Day allows organizations to raise a large amount of money quickly. This can be especially helpful for nonprofits with urgent needs or unexpected expenses.

2. **Engaging donors:** Giving day creates an urgency that can encourage donors to make a gift. It also allows organizations to connect with new donors and re-engage lapsed donors.

3. **Building community:** Giving day can create a community around a cause, with donors coming together to support a shared mission.

4. **Increasing visibility:** Giving Day can help raise awareness of an organization's mission through social media and other marketing efforts.

5. **Encouraging recurring giving:** Giving Day can serve as a launchpad for recurring giving programs, with donors who make a gift on giving day more likely to continue supporting the organization on a regular basis.

Peer-to-Peer Fundraising

Peer-to-peer fundraising mobilizes supporters to raise funds for an organization by creating their own campaigns and reaching out to their network for donations. Utilizing online platforms and social media, these campaigns leverage personal connections to inspire others to contribute. Incorporating competition and gamification, participants set goals, track progress, and receive incentives, fostering a sense of community. Examples include charity walks, runs, and crowdfunding campaigns. Peer-to-peer fundraising effectively generates funds, expands donor bases, and engages supporters as active participants in the fundraising process, tapping into the power of personal connections.

The following are important tips to consider to achieve your peer-to-peer fundraising goals:

#1. Organize your campaign

To kickstart your campaign, it is crucial to organize it effectively. Start by deciding on the type of peer-to-peer campaign that aligns with your organization's objectives. Consider your nonprofit's goals before selecting a campaign type, as certain campaigns may be more effective for specific goals than others. There are three main types of peer-to-peer campaigns:

- **Time-Based:** A time-based campaign has a defined start and end period, typically lasting a few weeks (although some may span up to a year). Usually, this type of campaign culminates in a significant event towards the end.

- **Rolling:** Rolling campaigns are not limited to a specific time frame, giving your organization the flexibility to take as long as necessary to achieve its fundraising objectives. However, this ensures the campaign maintains momentum and does not lose steam.

- **Giving Days:** As discussed earlier in this chapter, giving days are ideal for organizations that thrive on challenges. In a giving day campaign, the organization sets a fundraising goal within twenty-four hours, creating urgency and excitement. This type of campaign also presents a prime opportunity to leverage social media to amplify its reach and spread the message.

Consider your goals when deciding which type of campaign will likely work best for your organization.

#2. Choose your peer-to-peer fundraising software

Choosing the appropriate peer-to-peer fundraising software is a critical decision for any nonprofit, as it necessitates a solution that caters to all requirements while remaining within budget. With its donation and marketing capabilities, the peer-to-peer fundraising platform can determine the success or failure of your entire campaign. Therefore, selecting the appropriate provider should not be an afterthought. Take a closer look at your organization and its fundraising needs, and compile a list of desired features to help guide your selection process.

Below are some of the common features found in the most popular peer-to-peer fundraising solutions available today:

- Customization of giving forms
- Creation of team and individual peer-to-peer fundraising pages
- Ability to sell merchandise
- Availability of gamification tools such as fundraising badges and leaderboards

- Social media sharing capabilities
- Fundraising "thermometers" to track progress toward the goal
- Access to software training and technical support

#3. Recruit your supporters

Now that you've decided on the type of campaign you will run and have selected a reliable provider, it's time to recruit your supporters!

#4. Enable your supporters

One of the most critical steps in developing a successful peer-to-peer campaign is to equip your supporters with the tools they require to amplify their efforts, inspire others to join the cause, and become influential advocates for your organization.

To achieve this, your supporters will require the following resources:

- Personal coaching sessions
- Email templates for outreach
- Social media templates for sharing the campaign

- Acknowledgment templates for thanking donors
- Access to online training and technical support.

To effectively convey your message, including a story-related paragraph on every campaign page, accompanied by high-quality photos and/or videos and a compelling call to action, is crucial. Additionally, provide your supporters with a platform that simplifies the process of sharing why they are passionate about your nonprofit and cause. This will enable their friends, family, and acquaintances to comprehend your organization's mission better and become more motivated to contribute.

Giving Days have become a necessity for nonprofit organizations and educational institutions. Using online platforms has made it easier than ever to plan and execute these campaigns and reach new donors. With careful planning and execution, Giving Days, with a peer-to-peer strategy, can help organizations raise crucial funds, build community, and engage with supporters meaningfully.

Chapter 7:
The Future of Annual Giving

The world of annual giving is evolving, and technology is playing a crucial role in shaping its future. From online giving platforms to social media fundraising, nonprofit organizations are discovering new and innovative ways to engage with their supporters and raise funds.

One of the most significant changes in annual giving is the shift toward online giving platforms. These platforms allow donors to give directly to the organization through their website, making it easy and convenient for them to support the cause. Additionally, many of these platforms offer recurring and mobile giving features, making it even easier for donors to give regularly.

Another way technology changes the landscape of annual giving is through social media fundraising. Platforms like Facebook and Instagram now offer fundraising features allowing users to create campaigns and solicit donations from friends and followers. This has opened a new avenue for nonprofit organizations to reach new donors and raise awareness for their cause.

As technology evolves, we expect to see even more changes in annual giving. Here are some potential trends to look out for:

1. **Mobile Giving:** As more and more people rely on their smartphones for everyday tasks, we can expect to see an increase in mobile giving. Nonprofit organizations must ensure that their websites and online giving platforms are optimized for mobile devices to make it easy for donors to give on the go.

2. **Virtual Fundraising Events:** With the ongoing COVID-19 pandemic, many nonprofit organizations have had to cancel their in-person fundraising events. However, we have seen a rise in virtual events, such as virtual galas and charity walks. This trend will continue as organizations discover the benefits of hosting virtual events, such as increased accessibility and reduced costs.

3. **Artificial Intelligence:** AI is already used in the nonprofit sector to help organizations identify potential donors and personalize their outreach. In the future, we can expect to see even more advanced uses of AI in annual giving, such as predictive analytics and chatbots to answer donor questions and provide support.

4. **Blockchain Technology:** While still in its early stages, blockchain technology has the potential to revolutionize the way we give to charity. Blockchain allows for secure, transparent transactions, which could increase donor trust and reduce fraud. Additionally, blockchain could allow donors to track their donations and see how the organization uses their funds.

5. **Collaborative Giving:** Another trend we may see is collaborative giving, where multiple organizations come together to create a joint fundraising campaign. This could be particularly effective for smaller organizations that may not have the resources to run their campaigns.

6. **Pay Later:** The emergence of "donate now, pay later" fundraising platforms have become popular for non-profit fundraising. These platforms allow donors to donate to a charity or cause without paying immediately instead of deferring payment later.

7. **Digital Wallets:** Digitization of payment technology is the most significant trend in the nonprofit sector.

A 2020 study by Visa's Payment Panel revealed a 10% increase in credit card usage for charitable giving and a 20% decline in check giving over the last five years. With the proliferation of digital wallets such as Apple Pay, Google Pay, and Visa Direct, coupled with enhanced online donation experiences and QR code usage, individuals are increasingly donating online.

To inspire success in annual giving, nonprofit organizations must embrace the exciting possibilities that new trends offer and remember the fundamentals of effective fundraising. These fundamentals include cultivating solid relationships with donors, highlighting the impact of their contributions through compelling stories and visuals, and expressing prompt and sincere gratitude for their support.

As technology continues to shape the evolution of annual giving, the future looks bright for nonprofit organizations that can adapt and stay ahead of the curve in engaging with supporters and raising funds for their cause. The annual fund remains the lifeblood of any successful fundraising program, and it is crucial to actively participate in the action and keep your cause at the forefront of supporters' minds. By keeping up with current trends and leveraging exciting and engaging methods to involve supporters, your organization can stay in the spotlight and maintain its effectiveness in driving donations toward your cause.

Chapter 8:
Putting It All

Annual giving is not only the foundation of your giving program; it is the lifeblood of your program. It is only in annual giving that you can be quick and nimble. You have the power to identify donors who are ready for new programs to support. You can identify donors ready for that next step in their philanthropic journey.

An organization with a healthy annual giving program likely has a robust fundraising infrastructure. This includes effective donor stewardship, personalized communication strategies, and streamlined systems for processing and acknowledging donations. It showcases the nonprofit's commitment to donor-centered fundraising practices and its ability to manage donor relationships efficiently.

The advantage of a strong, robust annual giving program is that you can pursue scale. Keeping annual giving donors on major initiatives your organization is pursuing is critical to the success of your mission. Also, a strong and healthy financial position demonstrates legitimacy. Your organization will be seen as a stable, sustainable entity trusted by your constituents and external stakeholders.

Annual giving is a galvanizing force. This is an opportunity to communicate yearly sustainable impact while engaging board members and volunteers. An annual giving program serves as a fertile ground for nurturing major donors. By establishing a strong donor pipeline, organizations can identify individuals who have demonstrated a deep commitment to the cause and a capacity for increased giving. Consistent cultivation and recognition of annual donors lay the foundation for future major gifts, capital campaigns, and planned giving opportunities.

A thriving annual giving program brings together a community of passionate individuals dedicated to a shared cause. As more donors contribute, the collective impact grows exponentially. The sense of solidarity and shared purpose generated through annual giving inspires others to join, expanding the circle of support and influence. This broader community engagement creates a ripple effect that extends beyond financial contributions, mobilizing resources, expertise, and advocacy to address complex societal challenges.

www.ingramcontent.com/pod-product-compliance
Lightning Source LLC
Chambersburg PA
CBHW070124230526
45472CB00004B/1410